D1799345

Procrastination

Killed, Instantly

25 Proven Habits To Crush Procrastinating
And Achieve Double In Less Time

Angelo Zo

Table of Contents

Chapter One

—

Why Should You Listen to a Single Word I Say?
My story of Slogging it Out in the Trenches with the
P-Word (Procrastination)

I F YOU ARE READING THIS, then chances are… we have more in common than you might think.

You can fog a mirror (meaning you are human). You

eat, sleep and take care of business on the porcelain throne. And… wait for it…

You Procrastinate!

I know you know what I mean by that.

Chances are that it registers with visions of internet surfing, nervous eating bags of Cheetos, or maybe even visiting the dark corners of the internet that you know you probably shouldn't, all in lieu of an impending deadline for an important project.

Or maybe even worse!

Perhaps you don't have a deadline, which likely means that you are up a creek without a paddle.

Here's the thing…

if you have a pulse, then you also have the big, nasty procrastination gremlin constantly sitting on your shoulder; poking, prodding and teasing you with notions that are much more enjoyable than whatever it is that you are procrastinating from.

Why is this bad?

Simple because the tendency to procrastinate usually means that we have something important to do. Something that desperately needs to be completed.

Maybe it could be your thesis paper.
You know, that really important document that determines whether or not you obtain your Ph.D. which usually comes with a full YEAR to work on it, but instead you have put it off until the last MONTH and now you have to do it all in less than 30 days!

Or maybe it is that speech that you have to give in front of the board at work. They are all depending on you, you know. If you screw it up, your hag of a boss told you that you would undoubtedly be fired. But here you stand, looking at pictures of pristine beach houses in Key West for the past HOUR. You can't even afford any of them anyway!

What about that business that you were going to start so that you could get the hell out of dodge and tell your boss what you think of him as you cash in BIG? Have you even started it yet? Or are you aimlessly wandering down the career path instead of becoming an entrepreneur. Big difference.

I am all too familiar with this demon.
Procrastination, for all intents and purposes, was pretty much an (almost) un-curable addiction.

Here's my story (maybe you can relate):

By the grace of all that is good, I graduated college. Somehow. But at the time I was working part-time as a bartender.

I did not incline to change that either.
I enjoyed the social life. The free time that I got from no longer having to go to class was liberating. That just meant that I could sleep more. Relax, I did en masse. The perks (read: "free booze and a reason for attractive ladies to talk to you") were Excellent.
Long story short… I was the classic definition of a bum.

I knew that I needed a "real" job. My parents had no

problems consistently reminding me of that.

Truth be told… I wanted a better job.

I wanted to improve my life. I wanted to stop living off of my parents. For God's sake, I still got a monthly allowance because I couldn't pay the bills on my own!

Here I am. A college graduate aged 24 years (I took several "victory laps" to graduate), with a marketing degree still getting a monthly allowance like an 8-year-old would after he mows the lawn.

Humiliating.

I even had a mild case of clinical depression, for which I took medication. And yes. My parents paid for that too.

It was a vicious cycle.

I didn't ever apply anywhere because I was depressed. And, in turn, I was depressed because I didn't measure up to all of my buddies who went on to live the good life.

Good job. Good wife. Start a family. That whole thing.

Of course, I tried to apply for jobs. I even successfully applied to several.
But those went nowhere. Well… really only one led nowhere. I heard absolutely nothing from that one.

I received a call from the HR department of the other one. They said they wanted to set up a formal interview and that they would call back with available openings.

They didn't.

Still no job. So, I resorted to drowning my woes at the bottom of my pint glasses. For the record, beer does taste a little saltier when you add your tears.

The good thing about working at a bar is that you do meet a lot of people. And I didn't know it at the time, but by working at the bar, I ended up making a few solid connections.
Not too many, mind you. It is still a bar, and that scene doesn't necessarily attract the most ambitious of people.

Nonetheless, one fortuitous night, a man walked in that I had never encountered before.

I knew all of our regulars by name and, still living in the same small college town that I graduated college from, there weren't many new faces that walked in the bar. Especially during the summer months when school is out, and all of the students are visiting home.

This man didn't stand out much. There wasn't anything special about the way he dressed (t-shirt, jeans, and flip-flops).
And the only reason I even knew he walked into the bar is that I happened to be the bartender to serve him.

We got to chatting and, since I have the gift of gab, he took a liking to me.
It just so happened that he was the VP of engineering at a major defense company and was stopping in town to give a speech to the summer school kids at the college of engineering.

In other words, he was a bit of a big shot.

Long story, short, somehow, I got the guy liquored up enough to the point where he began to like me. He offered me a job at his company working as a market research analyst.

Mom and dad were thrilled. I was thrilled. Everyone was happy.

Except for one thing; my sloth ways continued to proliferate throughout my life.
And it didn't help that I HATED my new job. Hell, at least as a bartender you get to see something new each day.

But as a marketing analyst, watching paint dry, honestly, was better than this.

To make matters worse, I now had deadlines that I had to deliver on.

And if you are reading this, you are likely like me.

Try as I may, I could not get myself to start a project early and get ahead of the ball game. For the life of me, I could not do it.

Numbers required to be crunched. Files needed to be filed. Deadlines had to be met. And what did I do?

Not a damn thing. At least, not until the night before when panic would grip me around the throat and strangle me into an all-out anxiety attack.

At that point, I might finally take action.

Cracking open a can of sugar-free red-bull, I would pull all the necessary papers around me and get to work on what would, for sure, be an all-nighter.

But even while doing the actual assignment, the panic never left me. It would just ball-up and sit in the back of my throat, pulsing with every beat of my heart.
All the while, the negative self-talk raced through my mind.

It was always a most unpleasant experience.

Finally, upon the welcoming morning rays of sunlight, when I would undoubtedly still be working, I would wrap up whatever it was I was working on, sprint to work (usually still in the same clothes I sat down at my desk to work on).

I would also pray to whatever Gods there were that my boss wouldn't find out that I had pretty much BS'd my entire assignment.

Well, one day my boss did find out.

Based purely on my stupidity, I had left my browser window open on my office computer (another late-night brain fart).

I had copied and pasted my information from Wikipedia onto my word document and had left both the word document and the Wikipedia page open for all to see.

Apparently, plagiarism is bad. Whoops!

I was fired. And I hit a new low.

And after having my personal pity party by binge-watching Netflix and shotgunning Ben & Jerry's pints of Half-Baked ice cream, I had a tipping point.

Something had to be done.

I flipped open my computer, and for the next month, I pooled together the spare change I had left hiding in my couch cushions and purchased every single book I could find to cure my procrastination addiction.

No book was left unread.
No YouTube video was left unwatched.

Literally, everything that I could find on the subject, I absorbed like a sponge.

It paid off.

In this book, I have compiled only those tried and true tactics that I found worked wonders for me.

Just by implementing what I will later teach you in this book, in less than three months I was able to:

End my chronic procrastination habit once and for all

Start my own business

Land a smoking hot girlfriend (I pretty much got to choose between 4 girls, all of them prime candidates, and all of them wanted to date me.)

Match the same income I was initially making in my miserably dull office job, yet work less than HALF the hours

Write this very book that you are reading

Not too shabby for someone who, by all accounts was pretty much a bum by anyone's standards not even 90 days ago.

And here's the thing…

I'm not saying your results will be as dramatic as mine. But, I am suggesting that by implementing even just a handful of the tactics that I will teach you in this book, you can turn your life around in less than 90 days.

Chapter Two

—

What IS Procrastination?
The Truth Behind Productivity's BIGGEST Plague

S O, BEFORE WE GET INTO THE SOLUTION, the meat and potatoes so to speak, we first have to define the problem.

But what exactly IS Procrastination??

Let's start with something simple…

The Webster's definition of "Procrastination" is as follows:

"To put off intentionally and habitually"

Another definition that may fit the bill a little bit better is:

"to put off intentionally the doing of something that should be done."

That one is a little easier for most to understand. However, I want to draw your attention to something that both of these definitions have in common… They both place the control and the blame directly on YOUR shoulders.

Yep… that's right!

Procrastination, however you choose to define it in the

dictionary, is a personal decision. You are in control buckwheat!

This is both good and bad.

Unfortunate, because ultimately YOU are the cause behind why you have put off that particular thing that you have wanted to do for all of this time.

Bad, because the person looking directly back at you in the mirror is the one who is ultimately at fault for your predicament!
Sad, because no one else can fix your problem! Nope. Not one soul!

Let that sink in for a bit.

Now… the flip side of all of this is that you are also the solution!!

Because you are the one to blame, you are also the one that can fix it!
The ONLY one, in fact! And hallelujah for that!

But don't stress out if you believe that you are incapable of solving your own problem.

In fact, if you can still fog a mirror, then you can replicate my success.

Seriously. I can't pull a rabbit out of a hat. I don't have any super special skills (I can make a clover with my tongue if that counts?). I wasn't born with great genetics.

My family does not come from some long-lost royal bloodline that immigrated from Sudan.

I am not all that special, and yet I was still able to create what I would call a ringing success from literally nothing but blood, sweat equity, and a few tears.

Oh… and plenty of hours reading in the public library, googling the internet (that sounds odd) and tons and tons of time watching TED talks on YouTube.

But you don't have to do ANY of this because I have already done all the grunt work for you and condensed it into this lovely little volume that you can read in one sitting if you chose to do so.

And you should, because this stuff is life changing!

Ok. Now that I have gotten off of my soapbox, let's get back to the nitty gritty here.

For you to take control of this beast, it will help us to uncover a little more of the hidden truths as to what procrastination is and how it is caused.

And the truth is, it would seem, some are individuals are more prone to procrastination.

According to a study published in Psychological Science, which was conducted at Ruhr University Bochum, procrastination can be blamed mainly on the structure of two part of the brain.

These two parts have been identified as the amygdala and the dorsal anterior cingulate cortex (DACC, for short.)

The amygdala is responsible for those pesky little human things known as emotions.

It also happens to play a significant role in controlling our motivation. Specifically, the size of the amygdala determines our tendency to be either more emotion or more rational.

The DACC (I refuse to keep typing it out), essentially acts as a decoder for the amygdala and uses the information that the amygdala gives it to decide what actions the body will take.

It is also responsible for filtering distractions and competing emotions. Put plainly… this is the part of the brain that deals with procrastination. Think of it as the interpreter for the amygdala.

During this study, 264 individuals had their noggins scanned.

The scientists found that people with the annoying tendency to procrastinate usually had a larger amygdala along with a weaker connection between their amygdala and the DACC.

It would seem that people with a larger amygdala will more likely allow emotions to get in the way of rational thinking that people with a smaller amygdala.

Because of this, hesitation is more frequent in this population and causes them to put things off more. And, due to the uncertainty, procrastination will inevitably follow suit.

In other words, it would appear that you can blame your inability to turn in your homework on time to your amygdala.

But good luck convincing your teacher that it was the way your brain was formed that caused you to binge watch re-runs of cat videos on the internet.

Something tells me that will not fly. Although… it may very well be worth a try, if not for the entertainment value that it would bring.

So, if procrastination/s caused by the way your cranium is structured, would that imply that you are screwed to forever be average and put things off indefinitely?

Sorry… but you still don't have that as an excuse.

Even though this study would indicate a relationship

between brain formation and the tendency to procrastinate, scientists still argue that your own biology does not forever doom you.

In fact, the chief author of this study said that the brain is adaptive. In other words… it can change!

Weird, huh?

It turns out… since we, as humans, are living, breathing beings, we have the incredible ability to adapt to our surroundings and most stimuli that we are subjected to.

In other words, living organisms can adapt and change their biology to fit and mold to their surroundings.

In fact, this is not too unlike antibiotic-resistant bacteria. Initially, these particular bacteria were extremely susceptible to doses of medication.
But, over time and accompanied by frequent exposure to these antibiotics, the bacteria began to adapt to the drugs. Essentially, they began to evolve to be resilient, and eventually utterly resistant to the antibiotics.

Pretty cool, huh?

The human body reacts similarly. Of course, we are not single-celled microorganisms living in a parasitic relationship with other living beings.

However, as biological creatures, we do have the ability to adapt to our surroundings.

Tolerance to alcohol or drugs is an excellent example of this. Think of the very first time that you tried to sneak a drink from your parent's liquor cabinet (Just me? Weird…) Chances are, you began to "feel it" after no more than a few drinks.

In other words, you were a cheap drunk. But as the effects of college began to wear on you, and the number of parties you attended increased, your ability to digest and tolerate the effects of alcohol also began to rise.

The fact of the matter is, humans are incredible, adaptable creatures.

Don't believe me? Fine... then listen to Dr. Tim Pychyl, an expert on the matter out of Carleton University, Ottawa.

He was cited as saying during an interview with BBC, "Research has already shown that mindfulness meditation is related to amygdala shrinkage, expansion of the pre-frontal cortex and a weakening of the connection between these two areas."

Basically, what he is getting at is that the brain can change. And if your brain can change, then so can your procrastination habits.

Another argument in favor of human emotion being the culprit behind chronic procrastination says that we hesitate on taking action because we feel that we are not in the "right" mood to do it.

You can likely relate to this.

Often times, whenever I finally convince my naturally lazy self to sit down and get my work done, I feel restless. I am not motivated at that moment to do even one ounce of work. I feel stressed at the mere thought of just getting started.

In fact, rarely do I even actually feel in the mood to take the necessary action that my assignment calls for.

Perhaps you have experienced something similar.

Because of this emotional resentment to start a task, we get in the habit of convincing ourselves to just wait until our emotional state changes.
We just flat assume that we are going to be "in the mood" at some point.

Yet, that "some point" never comes. And thus, the constant spiral of procrastination takes root in our lives and manifests as a chronic issue.

We consistently believe that our emotional state has to match the current task at hand. But this couldn't be further from the truth.

Another study shows that procrastination can be

blamed on a thing known as "present bias." This idea essentially places your top priority on things or payoffs that are more tangible when considering the trade-offs between two future instances.

In other words, we tend to favor those things that give us instant gratification, and NOT those things that will pay off "someday."

A study performed at the University of Princeton scanned the parts of the brain responsible for making short-term and long-term decisions to test this idea of present bias.

They found that the options for short-term rewards light up the emotion part of the brain. The fascinating thing is that this will then override the abstract-reasoning areas of the brain.

In other words, if a cookie were to be placed directly in front of you, the chances are high that you would eat it.

In fact, if you really start to think about it... we are naturally hard-wired to procrastinate. The innate, hard-wired programming of any living organism is built purely for survival.

And pro-creation (but that is the subject of another book for another time.)

All living organisms have a very strong self-preservation mechanism.
This self-preservation mechanism recognizes and categorizes every single experience and every single moment as good or bad.

All good things strengthen the neural wiring in our brains to continue to seek out and find more of those "good things."

The opposite is true of all "bad things."

But the unfortunate reality is that in today's society, the things that our brain sees as "good," happen to be things like social media, alcohol, reality TV, sugar, your ex.

They appear "good," because they make us feel good. They relieve stress and allow us to decompress and relax.

And the "bad" things are anything that doesn't immediately give instant gratification.

Ironically enough, these would likely be the things that would propel you closer to your ultimate goals. Things like planning your day in advance, writing a little bit each day on that book, researching the necessary material you need for that paper that you have to write, putting together the slides for that all-important presentation.

You get the idea.

So, there is a bit of a paradox here.

Marketers have gotten savvy enough to appeal to this innate programming and are able to manipulate it into wanting to purchase all those things that actually encourage our procrastination habits.

Now, this isn't to say that the burden of the blame can be placed solely on society. It certainly doesn't help, but ultimately the power to change is with you, as the study on the amygdala above states.

But, as of this writing, over one-third of Americans feel dissatisfied with their lives. I am honestly shocked that it is not more. I suppose that we are a society content with under-achievement.

But hey, who am I to judge?

See, here's the thing… scientific studies aside, procrastination is KILLING you! As a human being, the most intelligent (arguably for some) being on the face of the earth, you have ideas and thoughts and assumptions that no one else on this earth has! You are unique!

So unique, in fact, that the odds of you even being born are 1 in 400 TRILLION!!

And here you sit, wasting your life away watching cat videos while you could be out doing incredible things!

The truth is, procrastination is so insidious in nature because it is the easy out.

It is the feel-good option between doing what you know you should and doing what is going to feel good in the now.

Procrastination is that voice that says "just wait a little longer until you feel like doing it. But right now, treat yourself instead. It's been a stressful day. You deserve it."

The truth is, however, that you will NEVER feel like doing those things that you need to.

Again, we tend to choose the path of least resistance. That, essentially, is procrastination in one sentence.

Think about kids… without the proper parenting, kids would choose the easy, feel-good things all the time and never choose the stuff that needs to get done.

"Do your homework and get off your Nintendo."

"Wash the dishes."

"It's time to go to bed."

"No. You can't have another bowl of ice cream."

Kids are the physical embodiment of procrastination and the parents are the guiding voice of reason that instructs them to become functioning adults.

However, as soon as we all turn 18, we no longer have that built-in parental system that tells us what needs to be done.

For many of us, as soon as we get out of the house, we have this moment of reckless abandon where we do ALL the things that we previously were unable to do under mom and dad's roof. And then, over time, we slowly learn that mom and dad were right.

We really do need to do the things we don't want to do if we truly want to live lives as functioning adults.

But where we stop is the moment when we feel we become "functioning adults" and then we slack off. We become just like everyone else.

We blend in with the statistical average that is society

and then we get depressed and upset because we ARE just like everyone else.

Pay the bills. Go to work. Get off on Friday. Relax a little. Repeat.

This is procrastination.

It is the societal norms creeping in on our lives and holding us to the standards that we are accustomed to. And any dreams of something more, of higher achievement, is cast aside as "weird."
And the reason we don't do anything to change it is that we, at some level, are O.K. with that notion.

Ultimately, curing procrastination is the changing of our own personal standards to a level of higher achievement.

And until we understand that, we will always be relegated to the norms of society. Stuck there just like everyone else.

As you read further into this book you will begin to

realize all the possible tips, tricks, and hacks that are available to you.

Chances are, not all of them will work for you. Nonetheless, I encourage you to try them (I mean… you never know until you try, right?)

Because until you do, you will never know what will work for you and what doesn't.

Life is one giant game of trial and error. Read an idea. Test it out. If it works, keep it! If it does not work, toss it out with the rest of the garbage.

And quite frankly, I do not know of any other way to learn.

In fact, please don't be one of those people that read this book, ordain themselves an "expert" on the matter, but don't do a single thing about it.

You need to go out and actually DO the thing. Meaning… you need to practice the techniques that I am about to teach you.

Anyone can read from a book. Anyone can claim to be an "expert."

But until you actually roll up your sleeves and get your hands dirty in the "taking action," part, nothing will happen for you.

That's how you use this book. All of the ideas in here have worked for me. I don't employ all of them every single day, but I pick and choose the ones that are most useful to me at the time.

I recommend you do the same.
In fact, I would be quite impressed if you were to do all of them at once.

Hell, you may even have other ideas.

Give it a try!
Because here is the deal… you will never beat procrastination and experience new levels of success in your life until you overcome the inertia keeping you where you have been up until now.

Have the courage to break free and try something new. It will take effort on your part. But just know that if I can do it, so can you.

You have read my story. Maybe you are in a better position than I was, maybe worse. But life is made one move at a time.

And the more moves you make in the right direction, the better your life will become.

That is just the truth.

Chapter Three

—

The 25 Timeless, Tested Habits to Beat Procrastination

#1

—

It's all in your head…
Change your mindset to change your life

Cliché, I know… But here's the deal. In the last chapter, we have already observed how procrastination is related to the structural integrity of the brain. I.E. the size of your amygdala usually determines whether or not you tend to be a chronic procrastinator.

BUT… Also remember that you can change your brain's structure and underlying chemistry through intentional meditation.

All of the studies surfacing on meditation have turned out nothing but copious positive effects that meditation has to offer and its effects on essentially curing procrastination are no different.

However, before you employ any tactics at all in this book, this one singular tactic (which is why I made it numero uno) is the factor upon which ALL other habits that follow will depend.

You need to draw the line in the sand NOW and commit to making a change.

Sure, it makes sense to be all hot and bothered (motivated) while you are reading this right now.

But what happens when it all hits the fan? Life has a not-so-pleasant way of kicking us in the teeth when we least expect it to. How will you react?

Will you be resilient and hold steady in your commitment to defeating procrastination, no matter what?

Your frame of mind will ultimately make or break you in these instances. Will you crumble? Or will you wholeheartedly embrace what I have to say and what follows in these pages?

Mindset is everything. The only question remaining is… will you make the switch and embrace the process?

#2

—

Treat Time Differently

What is the most valuable asset in the world? Mountains of gold? Stashes of silver bullion? Could it be stock or bonds in the most profitable companies in the world? Perhaps governmental power?

I'll give you a hint… it is none of these.

Give up yet?

It's time!

Yes, those little subtle ticks of the clock as each second passes are the most precious asset available on earth.

Why?

Simple. Even as you have read these sentences, I have essentially stolen valuable time away from your life.

You will never get them back. They are forever gone; lost in the fabric of time and space. And until we invent time travel, those moments can never be repeated.

Successful people truly get this.

Billionaire businessmen, professional athletes, Ph.D. candidates. All of them understand the value of time. They know that each moment can never be retrieved and because of it, they go to incredible extremes to remind themselves of this.

Perhaps you have heard the term: "Make each second count?"

There is no truer line.

And here's the game-changer… we all have the same amount of time!

The difference between the super successful and, well, YOU… is that the successful people are actually taking action on each and every second that they possibly can.

I've even heard of successful entrepreneurs literally pasting the number "1440" everywhere across their office.

That number is sacred to them. It happens to be the number of minutes available in a day.

How are yours being used?

Do you spend your time daydreaming and watching cat videos on YouTube? Or are you taking action?

Choose wisely.

#3

—

What is Your "ONE THING?"

Gary Keller is the man in charge of Keller-Williams Realty. As of this writing, it is the largest real estate franchise in the United States.

In terms of business success, you could make the convincing argument that It is on the level of Wal-Mart, in terms of pervasiveness in the United States.

Just about everyone has seen the iconic "KW" signs in red lettering; likely in their very own neighborhood when a house has been put up for sale.

But what is the reason for this incredible success? Long hours at the office? Deep pockets? A lucky break?

Far from it. The thing that Mr. Keller attributes his incredible success to is by unrelenting, ruthless elimination of everything except for "THE ONE THING."

To find this one thing, he uses what he calls the focusing question.

This question guides his decision making to eliminate everything except for the only thing that essentially acts like the first domino in a line of successive dominos.

The idea is that once you knock over that one domino, the rest fall on their own in rapid succession. This is referred to as the domino effect.

The question is as follows:

"What is the ONE THING I can do, such that by doing it everything else will become easier or unnecessary?"

He adds to this by adding that "most people struggle to comprehend how many things don't need to be done if they would just start by doing the right thing."

Once you have found your one thing, you should immediately drop everything else and focus disproportionate amounts of time on that one thing until you experience a domino effect.

#4

—

Morning Magic Time

Have you ever felt as though you run around like a chicken with your head cut off all day and the only thing that you get done is a whole lot of nothing'?

I have, every day, as soon as everyone else wakes from their peaceful slumber; there is a buzz of activity in the air. And that buzz is the constant cry for attention by every living thing with a pulse.

Seriously. Think about it. Especially if you are in a position of authority, you get requests ALL. DAY. LONG for stupid, trivial matters that really don't take much brain power to solve.

And yet, here you are as your lowly employee comes in to tell you that the printer is out of ink. But not to worry! He already ordered another cartridge from Amazon using overnight shipping. It will be here by morning.

And while he drained several heartbeats from your life force telling you absolutely USELESS information that didn't matter one iota, he then proceeds to pull out his phone and show you pictures of his new chihuahua that he got last night. His name is Spencer.

Tick-tock.

He just continues to waste your time. And this is a mild situation, yet things like this happen every day. And there seems to be no end to the numerous fires that you "just have to" put out each day.

But guess what... even though you have no control over other people's actions, you can put yourself in a position to get all of your important tasks done and out of the way without any of these "time vampires" to suck you dry.

I would like to refer you to the morning.

Ahh, the morning. That blissful time of day when everyone else is asleep, leaving you free to focus and be at your most productive.

I absolutely love this tactic. In fact, it is responsible for a huge portion of my success in killing my procrastination demons.

During this time, I make it a priority to complete my most important activity first. By doing this as soon as I wake up, I leave myself distraction-free and also free of other people's problems and personal distractions so that I can get my work done.

Now, I would encourage you to wake up with the chickens. Ideally, wake up when it is still dark outside. This ensures that just about every other person will be soundly asleep. You will receive no text messages. No phone calls. Just pure, unadulterated bliss for you to focus on your most important work.

#5

—

*Create Your Environment for Peak
Productivity*

Lots of things stress me out. I tend to be about as wound up as a cat. Always high strung. Always on edge.

This is another reason why the morning magic tactic works so well for me. It also happens to tie in wonderfully with this tactic as well. And that is to create your environment for peak productivity.

As I have already mentioned. There is not a lot that you can do to control other people's actions. But you can take matters into your own hands.

If you can create a space that eases your stress and puts you "in the mood" for getting work done, all the better!

And it is actually pretty fun.

As I write this, I currently sit in my own personal home office. There are absolutely ZERO electronics. On the walls, I have plenty of not-so-subtle reminders of wealth that include pictures of gold bars, framed $100-dollar bills, and more clocks than I can currently count in order to remind me that time is a-ticking!

These are all very intentional tactics that I employed in order to optimize my environment for peak productivity and I highly advise you to do the same.

Now, everyone's personal space is going to vary from person to person. However, the important thing is that the things that you choose to surround yourself with are used as fodder to get the creative juices going and squeeze every ounce of productivity possible out of your noggin.

I ditch all electronics because if I have a computer or a smartphone, I will inevitably grab them and perform mindless searches on things that do not matter, wasting precious time and energy.

Your environment matters. I have even seen such extremes as people sound-proofing their doors and walls. I do not feel that this is necessary for me, but you may find it useful.

Nonetheless, the whole point is that you create your

own personal space, free from distractions. It should be peaceful and should be the place you go to hole yourself up in whenever you need to get some serious work accomplished.

#6

—

Time Blocking

Since you and I are both human, that likely means that you and I have a tendency to be a slave to our calendar. All too often, we receive demands on our time (wanted or unwanted.)

It can be as harmless as a friend asking you to go to a movie, to a bit more insidious like a boss requiring you to work over the holidays.

Maybe you have told someone else that you will "pencil them in?"

I eventually got the realization that, even though I was beginning to become more organized, upon looking at my calendar I noticed that most of my appointments had absolutely NOTHING to do with me or my own personal goals.

No freakin' wonder that I wasn't making any advances in my life!

That's when I discovered time blocking. Each morning, usually during my morning magic hours, I am sure to block out large chunks of time for numero uno (me). These "time blocks" are intervals of time reserved solely for me. Essentially, it is an appointment that I choose to keep with myself.

I treat them just as though I would an appointment with my boss or an important client. It is immovable, come hell or high water.

If you employ this tactic (and you should), you need to be cautious that you DO NOT give in to the temptation to let others infringe on your own personal time.

I would use this tactic to ensure that I got my workouts in. I would block off one hour of time, 3 days per week at 5 PM.

This was my time that I spent at the gym working on myself.
At the time, my boss requested that I attend a meeting that evening, which would cut my workout short.

I politely told him that I was already booked for that

time. He didn't ask why. I didn't give him a reason.

You don't need one either. An appointment set for you is vastly more important than one set for someone else's priorities anyway. Don't feel bad for keeping the appointments that you make with yourself.

Use this tactic for ALL important tasks. Projects. Personal development. Constructive reading. Block off chunks of time to work on you and your own personal skills.

This is what will make you better over the long haul.

#7

—

33-Minute Intervals

Have you ever sat down for hours at a time to knock out a project, only to feel incredibly fatigued and exhausted at the end of it all?

I certainly have.

Here's the thing. I HATE working for hours on end. I have no earthly idea how people do it, and I have a theory that no one does. In fact, studies have shown that our focus is limited, and we only have the ability to maintain high levels of focus for 33 minutes at a time.

So, what do I do? I only work for 33 minutes at a time.

Now… I'm not saying that I only work for 33 minutes per day. No, no, no… That would be nuts. I am saying that I only work in 33-minute intervals. And once that interval is up, I put down my pen, stand up, and walk around for a bit. At this point, I take a 5 to 10-minute break of doing whatever I please. I watch cat videos. I play with my dog. Whatever I feel like doing, I do in that time period.

Once that 5-minute rest is up, I am back at work, ass on the chair, and focused as can be.

What this does is it breaks large projects up into manageable bits. I have a hard time trying to focus as it stands, much less if I work non-stop. But by breaking my working time into 33-minute intervals, I not only maintain a high level of focus, but I also am able to get more done.

#8

—

First Things First

I had touched on this a little bit earlier when I mentioned the morning magic tactic. But now I would like to go a little more in depth on this topic.

In the book by the great Stephen Covey, "The 7 Habits of Highly Effective People", he mentions that successful people "put first things first."

This basically amounts to having your priorities straight. If you are a writer, your "first thing" that you need to put first is well, writing!

If you own your own business, then your "first thing" that you need to do first is making sure that it is profitable.

Businesses need sales to survive. So, you need to be making sure that you are making consistent sales.

Doing these items first matters. Inevitably we all have a freakin' laundry list of things that we need to do and require our attention.

But there aren't quite so many things that are truly important for moving the needle on our goals.

Those are the things that need to get first priority during the day.

And usually, that thing which needs to be done first is usually the most uncomfortable and has the highest propensity to be put off.

Don't fall into that trap!

Do your most important and most difficult task first thing in the day!

Tim Ferriss, the author to the "The 4-Hour Work Week," has a great productivity tool. He writes out everything that he needs to get done for that day on a little 3x5 index card.

After he has listed everything that needs to get done, he goes down the list and makes his selection based on the following question:

"what 3 items would make me feel like a success at the end of the day if those were the only things that I completed?"

Everything else then becomes a distraction until he finishes those top 3 items. Only then will he work on the other things.

#9

—

Do the First 10 Minutes

Sometimes starting is the hardest part. Yet, after those first agonizing moments of action, I begin to settle into the task and achieve my peak state of productivity. After that moment, it is all downhill and the work just becomes part of my natural routine.

You see… we humans are curious creatures. We have a terrible habit of making a bigger deal out of things than they need to be. And in doing so, we torture ourselves in the anticipation of the pain of the activity.

Yet, once we actually take a deep breath, calm ourselves, and just sit down to do the work, it turns out that the pain was all just that… nothing more than a made-up manifestation of the anticipation of the activity. The actual activity itself was really not so bad.

Think about that time back in high school when you put off that project until the last few days just because every time you thought of the idea of sitting down and actually knocking some of it out, your stomach would somersault. Therefore, waiting "just one more day" wouldn't really set you back that much… Except, when you add "just one more day" over multiple occurrences, you get several days of lost time and productivity.

So how do you overcome this?

I have adopted this tactic to trick myself into doing the work. If can just work for a solid 10 minutes and just start, then I usually end up working for much longer periods of time than that 10 minutes.

Inertia is a powerful thing. You know that whole law of physics that says, "An object in rest or motion will stay in rest or motion until acted upon by an outside force."

This timeless principle applies to productivity as well.

So, if you can just force yourself into sitting down and cranking out the first 10 minutes of work, inertia says that you will continue to sit there and work for a much longer period of time.

#10

—

Fill your Calendar

I have heard a quote a while back that says:

"If you want to meet the devil, leave white space on your calendar."

Let's use the devil as a metaphor here for procrastination and lack of productivity. I have found it to be true that as soon as I am sitting around on my bum with nothing to do, I tend to dive into self-destructive activity.

This can be seemingly harmless such as watching Netflix or maybe even drinking a beer or two.

But If you lack organization in your life and you spend the majority of your time on non-productive and non-meaningful tasks, you will begin to become that kind of person.

We are creatures of habit. It won't be long before your days consist of nothing but binge-watching re-runs of Netflix shows and a dabble into alcoholism.

Humans like routine. So be very careful what your routines consist of.

Knowing this, make sure that your days are chocked full of productive activities. Make sure to include plenty of time blocks for important tasks. Give yourself a 5 to 10-minute break in between periods of 33 minutes of focus.

For the love of all that Is good, make sure that the majority of your days are filled with pre-planned, pre-determined activities that will move you forward towards your goals. And make sure that you stick with your appointments like glue.

Otherwise, you will meet the devil in his many forms. And he does have a lot of them.

#11

—

Apply the Parkinson's Law

"Work expands to fill the time available".

In other words, if you assign yourself 7 days to complete a given 2-hour task, such task, according to Parkinson's Law, will increase in complexity to fill the given time.

The caveat to this rule is that most people often apply this unknowingly.

Did you ever have a deadline for a project where you waited until the last possible moment to start your work on it?

At that point, you then take a task that was originally supposed to be worked on over the duration of a week, and you condensed it into the last couple of hours before it was due.

You didn't spend a full week's worth of time working on that project. Instead, you spent maybe 6-8 hours of time actually working on it. And all of those hours were likely just before the project was due.

But all through the week, you likely had these grand plans of how to make this project the very best it could possibly be. Yet, when it came down to crunch time, likely all of those little details were tossed, and you focused solely on the details of the project that were absolutely essential.

This is the idea of self-imposed deadlines. But not just any deadline. When you take on a task, think of the amount of time that it will take for you to complete the task, then, try cutting that time in half and attempt finishing it within that edited timeline.

Admittedly this is difficult to do. However, if you can swing it, the amount of time you save will be unrivaled.

#12

—

Create a Starting Ritual

As I have mentioned before, humans are creatures of habit. We love and thrive in routine.

But the opposite is also true. We don't do all that well in situations we are unfamiliar with. Change is not our friend.

So, using this psychology, we can manipulate ourselves into high levels of productivity by creating a starting habit, or ritual.

Habits rely on certain cues. Once these cues are triggered, the waterfall of events that happens next is almost effortless.

In fact, scans of the human brain have shown that activities that can be defined as a habit require dramatically less brain wave activity than do other activities.

So, our goal would be to create a habit of working.

And we do this by creating a starting ritual. For me, this is as simple as turning on the coffee maker, making myself a cup of coffee, sitting at my desk and putting my earbuds in.

All of this happens the very same way, each and every morning when I sit down to get my work done.

#13

—

Don't Break the Chain

If you can habitualize what you do, you will be much more likely to achieve incredible success.

For example, comedian Jerry Seinfeld supposedly had an incredibly simple method for coming up with his jokes.

When a young man asked what his secret was for immeasurable success as a comedian, he replied by instructing that person to go get a large wall calendar. Seinfeld then assigned the man to write a joke every day. As soon as that joke was written, the man was to place a large red "X" on that day of the calendar. Over time, a pattern of X's would emerge, resembling a chain.

Seinfeld's top rule for success… don't break the chain.

Mr. Seinfeld is reportedly worth over $860 million dollars. To put that in perspective, Tom Cruise is at a measly $460 million…

So here is the key to massive success, a la Seinfeld… show up every day and work on your craft. Jerry has said that everything began to change for him when he observed a shift of construction workers returning to work after a lunch break.

He then thought that if these guys, doing some of the most physically demanding, blue-collar labor around, could show up every day and do their job, then so could he.

He went from working on his comedy routine 1-2 times per week to treating it like a full-time job, writing jokes and improving his routine every single day.

Take a page out of his book. Don't break the chain!

#14

—

Get Rid of Digital Distractions

I hate my smartphone with an unbridled passion. I wholeheartedly believe that the thing is the spawn of Satan, brought up from the fiery depths of hell to forever doom civilization.

Seriously.

All the notifications. The pings. The dings. It is enough for me to have rolled down the window of my car and chuck the thing as far as I could fling it while going down the highway at 70 miles per hour. Yes… I did this…

And the damndest thing happened. For the next week that I was without a phone, my productivity shot through the roof!

I'm serious. Apart from my closest friends and family thinking I was dead because I did not respond to my phone, I achieved the most productive week I have ever had. No comparison.

And here's why:

I no longer had the constant, unyielding distraction of other people vying for my attention. No more did I have to figure out other people's problems. No more did I waste 45 minutes to an hour at a time listening to my mother droll on about how my brother needs to get his act together.

I was free.

And the only reason that I ended up breaking down and buying another phone was that I had a client phone conference coming up. And this client accounted for something like 35% of my total income at the time.

Kind of important.

However, from that point forward, I imposed ruthless phone rules on myself.

I only talk on the phone during pre-appointed times. I do not have ANY social media apps on my phone. In fact…. I deleted every app that I possibly could. I do not have my email linked to my phone.

The ONLY person that is allowed to reach me is my girlfriend. That is it. Otherwise, even my own mother has to make a phone appointment.

If I have to check email, I do it at pre-scheduled times on my computer and only for 25 minutes at a time. I guard my email address like a miser and only give it out to important clients.

I'm serious as a heart attack. Just by limiting my interaction with electronic devices and being extremely cautious when I do interact with them, I am able to uphold an incredibly productive working life where I get more done than most of my peers, combined!

These rules may seem stringent to you. But I encourage you to give it a go. It is the most liberating feeling to not be at every single human's beck and call 24/7.

#15

—

Re-Start your Day at 2 P.M.

I admittedly do not always like to do this one. But it does do wonders during times when I am my most busy. Also, it helps whenever I slack off a bit in the morning or use that time to go on a breakfast date with the girlfriend.

But think of it this way… We have already discussed how useful the morning time is for peak productivity. No one is around to bother you/call/text you and you can spend the time you have while the rest of society is dead to the world to get your most important tasks done.

But sometimes you just need a little extra "morning" magic to get the job done. Therefore, every now and then I turn the afternoon, specifically the time around 2 P.M., into my second morning.

Now… due to the lack of distraction, the true morning time still reigns as king. But if you can shift 2 P.M. into your second wave of productivity, you can, essentially, double your productivity.

The catch here is that you will have to construct a "dead zone" where you are essentially "dead" to the world. No one should be able to contact you. No one should be able to find you. You need to have a designated "hiding spot" that you can escape to.

I say this because if you were to stay at work, distractions will come at you as if they were the next great flood of biblical times. Co-workers, employees, bosses, and clients will all pile work on top of your desk and expect you to stop whatever it is that you are doing and bow to their "supreme" wishes.

Therefore, once you begin your second morning in the early afternoon, you will need to find a spot, away from all distractions, where you can bunker down and try to simulate your morning magic.

It works well… IF you can truly get away. This will take some experimenting with your different locations.

But the payoff can potentially be double your productivity!

#16

—

Take a Break

Sometimes we need to just relax and let the ol' noggin catch a break.

We can't just go, go, go all the time and not eventually expect some kind of catastrophic cranial melt-down.

Think of it like our cars. You can't just continually drive it forever, for days on end without stopping to refuel. Eventually, after so many miles of pounding the pavement, you will need to stop and get the oil changed, the tires rotated, and the car tuned up. Otherwise, you would be lucky if your car lasted more than a year or two.

The same is true for us. We need time to relax. Time to breathe. Time to play. We are inherently social creatures that thrive on interaction with other humans. We can't just hole ourselves up, hunched over a computer forever and expect us to be able to function like a normal human being.

We need time for play. This takes our mind off of work

and allows the batteries to re-charge.

Now… it may seem weird that I am advocating you taking an intentional break from working in the middle of a book about how to not procrastinate. But hear me out… as long as you are following at least some of the other tactics that are listed out in this book, this particular tactic will actually increase your productivity; not decrease it.

So, invite some friends over. Go see a movie. Take a walk with the dogs.

Honestly, some of my best ideas and biggest breakthroughs have come when I have forced myself to take a break from work.

Just remember…'' All work and no play make Jack a dull boy.''

#17

—

Enlist Accountability

Oftentimes we procrastinate on things that are important purely because we don't have anyone to hold our feet to the fire.

Accountability is a game changer.

Think about it this way:

We have no issue completing projects for school or work. Whenever there is an impending deadline looming in the future where we will have to answer to someone else, we tend to get moving. Perhaps not until the last minute… but at least we get it done (usually.)

But when it comes to our own endeavors… no dice.

How is that business coming that you have been planning to start for the past three years? What about that book that you were going to write? You got half-way through the introduction and then… nothin.'

You had no one to answer to. No one to put the

squeeze on you. No one that you would let down if the project went unfinished (other than yourself.)

But when you get others involved, you put the pressure on yourself, because now you have someone to answer to. Now someone else will know of your failures if you choose to continually procrastinate.

This form of social pressure works wonders.

Personally, I posted updates on my projects on Facebook. EVERYONE knew what was going on in my life. The things I was working on. The stumbles that I had.

This also meant that people would ask me how things were going. I had to pony up. You can only lie so much before people figure out that you are a phony.

The upside to this is tremendous, however. I finished that particular project in record time!

#18

—

Inflict Personal Pain

I have done this one a few times before when I truly need something to get done A.S.A.P.

Here's the idea behind it:

You and someone else (it can be a friend or a foe. In fact, it may work better with someone you don't like very much), will draw up a legally binding social contract.

One way would be to word it in a manner that you will pay your friend/enemy a certain, pre-determined amount of money if you fail to complete the required task on time.

An alternative method would be to write the contract where you receive some kind of very unpleasant punishment in return for failing to complete the task.

I have heard of such extremes such as people organizing matches with professional boxers as punishment.

And, yea… of course the person being punished knows absolutely NOTHING about boxing.

There is a lot of psychology at play here though. Humans will naturally avoid anything that is deemed painful. Usually… the task that you are procrastinating on is considered to be painful. Therefore, if you can leverage pain in such a way that the punishment is MORE painful than the thing which you are procrastinating on, then you will manipulate yourself into completing the task within the predetermined time.

This one can be considered to be a little extreme, however desperate times call for desperate measures.

And no one can argue the effectiveness of this method. I have not known it to fail very often. So, if you TRULY want to take your productivity to levels that are off of the charts… bring this idea up to a very vindictive soul; someone with enough creativity to keep you awake at night and working on your appointed task.

#19

—

Use Tools to Aid in Eliminating Distraction

There's an app for everything these days. This is both good and bad. I'll start with the bad.

With things like Candy Crush and Plants vs. Zombies (seriously?), people have made absolutely disgusting amounts of money preying on the easily distracted attention of others. And I'll even admit to succumbing to a few games of Tetris. As of this writing, I believe the rage is a game known as "Fortnight." I could have misspelled that, but I would not know as I have never played it.

But the point here is that you need to tread carefully in the world of electronics and the internet. There are just too many things constantly jockeying for your attention, and if you are not careful you will waste gobs of time wasting away precious minutes that you will never get back. And the only thing you will have to show for is an empty pocket and increased skill at menial games that will never matter.

Now. There are other apps that can actually aid in your

quest for optimal productivity and the slaying of procrastination.

A very helpful one that I use is one called "Freedom." This internet app can be used to block you from internet access for pre-determined amounts of time.

I use this one whenever I have a major writing project to do. Chances are, If I have access to the internet at my fingertips, it will only be a matter of time before I aimlessly begin the dreaded "surfing."

But with the freedom app engaged, I am just not even able to pull up my browser. I am permanently blocked from the internet for up to 8 hours at a time. And this includes my smartphone as well.

It is a game changer that delivers HOURS of productivity back to me each and every day.

#20

—

Make and Use Lists

There have often been times that I have been in "the mood" of getting things done, and yet, I just can't seem to remember what it is that I need to do at that time.

Here's the thing… so much activity happens each and every day in our lives that there is absolutely no possible way on this green earth that we can remember it all in our heads. Albeit, some are scary good at remembering most things. But I have yet to meet a man (or woman) that did not have that gut-wrenching sinking feeling in their stomach when they realize that they have forgotten an incredibly important task.

This could have easily been avoided by keeping a simple list of things to do. And it doesn't have to be fancy. Mine is a 5x8 yellow legal pad. Every time I remember a task that needs my attention, I just jot it down on the front page. Whenever I finish that task, I just put a strike through that item. Apart from being efficient, it is also very satisfying.

I have tried keeping my list on my phone in the notes

section. It just doesn't work quite as well. And inevitably, every time that I do refer to my list (which wasn't very often), I would click through all the other applications and eventually end up on Facebook, where I wasted EVEN MORE time looking at the highlight reel of everyone that I never talk to anymore (so glad I deleted that from my phone.)

Besides, keeping it on a physical pad that I carry with me keeps these tasks at the front of mind, and hence I get to them in a much more efficient and timely manner.

Just by using a physical to-do list, I have found my tendency to procrastinate has been significantly diminished.

#21

—

The 'Suck-It-Up' Method

Sometimes getting through unproductive slumps just requires a swift kick to the nethers to get your tail in gear and actually get your work done.

The reality is that I am hardly ever motivated to do my work. In fact, I believe it was American author Kurt Vonnegut who once proclaimed that he felt like an armless, legless man with a crayon in his mouth every time he sat down to write.

And this is one of the most successful authors in American literature saying this!

The point is this… if we always waited for rosy feelings of motivation, drive, and productivity, society would crumble and likely implode on itself because NOTHING would ever get done.

I even consider writing a passion of mine, and yet, every single time I sat down to pound out the manuscript for this book, a feeling of dread boiled up from within.

Every time I sit down to write, my procrastination demons rear their ugly head, tempting me back to my old ways. I have to beat them back with a metaphorical pole in order to continue my streak of productivity.

And this is life. Oftentimes, you just have to suck it up, put your ass in the chair and force yourself to work whether you want to or not. Oftentimes, you will not want to work. And that is just the cold, hard truth.

If you are one to only work when inspiration strikes, you will go hungry. Just as I did.

#22

—

Avoid the Rush-Hours

I HATE traffic. Almost as much as I hate my smartphone. It really is a close battle for first place here sometimes.

Really, ever since I broke away from my old lifestyle, the notion of wasting even a single second is absolutely nauseating to me. Hence the reason why sitting in traffic is less appealing to me than a sharp stick to the inner ear.

Just out of curiosity, I looked up the amount of time that people spend in traffic each year. The number almost made me wet myself:

42 HOURS!

Calculated out over a lifetime, that would amount to over 100 days sitting on your bum behind the wheel!

Ridiculous!

So much wasted time. So much wasted potential. To

further give myself that time back, I make it a point to avoid the busy times as much as possible. This would include the early morning and lunch hour rushes along with the 5 O'clock traffic time. I won't eat lunch anytime from 11:30 to 2 P.M.

If I am eating out, I make the reservations over the phone to avoid waiting. In that case, I ask for an ETA and then I will head over.

I pre-book times for appointments with the doctor, hair stylist, dentist, and any other appointment-based service. If these people are constantly "behind schedule," I find someone else to obtain my desired services from.

I just flat refuse to give myself any reason to waste time. Especially since I have already done enough of that in my early years of employment.

This may be a tad extreme for some, and it certainly gives me weird look from family and friends. However, my bank account is also much higher than theirs, so I have no issues sleeping at night.

#23

—

Minimize Un-Planned Activity

How many times have you woken up and you immediately have 2 missed calls from your boss, 3 texts from your mother asking if you are still alive, and an inbox full of emails, mostly from Amazon suggesting brand new books you might enjoy because you bought "50 Shades of Gray?"

You are doomed from the start to constantly react to other people's whims and wishes, leaving your plans on the back burner, only to be glanced at once society has finished chewing you up and spitting you out.

Ain't nobody got time for that! Especially if you have the yearnings for booting procrastination.

The last thing you need is a bunch of other wind-suckers (people) helping your procrastination habit along.

So, here's the solution... you should have already planned your day in advance, woken up early to take advantage of your morning magic time, time blocked and determined your top priority (your one thing) for the day.

Now comes the part where you have to beat back all the time vampires (people) with a wooden stake and a necklace of pungent garlic cloves.

If you let them, the people around you will toss all of their unwanted chores on your plate of things to do, simply because they are too lazy to do it themselves and they too, have a nasty procrastination habit.

You CANNOT let them if you want these tactics to work.

Your new favorite word, in order to minimize unplanned activity, should be a hard, swift "NO!"

That one simple word is the cure-all for your unplanned activities.

In fact, if you can make that your knee-jerk response to every request that is tossed your way (and there will be plenty!), you will have more time to focus on things that matter than you will believe.

This tactic is the one that gives all your other procrastination-killing tactics a fighting chance. If you take anything away from this book at all, let it be this:

Learn to say "no" to anything and everything.

Doing this will protect your ability to become and stay productive on the things that matter, ultimately killing procrastination

#24

—

AVOID AT ALL COSTS!

Warren Buffett, ultra-successful investor and often-times the point man on the list for richest people in the world, has an incredible tactic for killing procrastination and optimizing your time. So naturally, I offered a curious ear to his advice and promptly stole (borrowed) his advice and put it to use in my own life.

It is as follows:

Make a list of everything that you want to accomplish and have in your life. Write down everything and leave nothing behind. What do you want to accomplish? Where do you want to travel? Do you want to own a house in the Florida Keys? Do you want to become a successful businessman (or woman)? Want to start your own non-profit? Write a book? Get your Ph.D.?

Whatever little idea pops into your cranium, scribble it down on paper. And keep writing until you have 25 items on your list (or more.) If you are like me, you may find that it is difficult to write down 25 items. But nonetheless, make sure you have 25.

Now… once that is accomplished, take the time to comb through your list and circle the top 5 items on your list. Those things that you want above all others.

Now, here's the kicker… the other items that did not get circled, these now become your "avoid at all costs!" list.

Seriously… I know that these things are things that you want to accomplish in your life. But Warren's argument is that we are trying to do too much at once. Once you figure out the crucial few items that you desire, you put all your eggs into those baskets.

I'm not saying never go for the other items. Instead, I AM saying that you need to put all your effort into accomplishing only those first 5 before you ever consider doing anything else.

#25

—

Stop to Think

Here's one that really gets my blood boiling and moves me into instantaneous and fervent action…

Sit down for just a moment and I want you to think. Think about all of the successful people in the world. More specifically… think about the people that have already done what you want to do.

Inevitably, I would bet that there are some individuals that you consider "unfit" for the level of success that they have.

For example… I was talking with a clinical psychologist the other day and the name "Dr. Phil" came up. Immediately he had a look creep across his features that looked as though someone was waving a steaming dog turd under his nose.

"I HATE that man! He has no clue what on earth he is talking about and yet, there he sits on national TV making the big bucks while I'm struggling to pay rent!"

Life isn't fair ladies and gents.

But here is the good news. I've been in his situation before. And it always made me cringe to think of the people that have already accomplished what I am trying to do because most of these people seem as though they can't even tie their own shoelaces in the morning!

However, instead of getting angry at them and at your circumstances, use that anger as fuel. Think about it this way:

"If someone who is that stupid can do this, then so can I!"

It works like a charm. Never once have I sat on my tail and moaned about how unfair life is whenever I think of the complete idiots that have already accomplished what I want to do.

Bonus #1

—

Tie Everything to your Goals

Jim Rohn, a famous businessman and motivational speaker, states that the reason there aren't more millionaires in this world is that people don't have enough reasons to be.

Certainly, it is not for lack of opportunity! For goodness sake, just look at some of the ridiculous things people have gotten stinkin' rich off of!

Things like the squatty potty, the shake weight, and even reality television (spare me, please!).

So why aren't more people rich? Easy… they just don't have enough reasons to be.

Similarly, I would contend that the reason why more people aren't as productive as they want to be is that they do not have enough reasons to be. And this is why you have to fight, tooth and nail, to link your reasons for being productive to your ultimate goals.

You need to constantly be thinking:

"Is what I am doing this very instance, moving me closer to, or further away from my goals?"

Now this question also implies that you have clear goals. If your goals are clear as mud, in other words, you really don't know what you want... then this is your first assignment. Get your goals down on paper, on purpose and make sure that they are set in a way that allows you to pursue them.

Now, this book is not about setting goals, but it IS dependent on you having goals that are already well-set.

If you do not know how to set proper goals, then you need to do the research to find out how. Hint: Jim Rohn would be a good place to start!

Bonus #2

—

Take Advantage of "Inconvenient" Time

We all have those moments of just "awkward" amounts of time.

This could be the downtime between appointments, sitting at the airport waiting for your flight, or, God help you… sitting at the DMV.

Whatever the instance, instead of whipping out your phone and watching "epic fail" videos on YouTube or scrolling through Facebook, why not use that time for something productive?

Here's an idea… read a book! Books have all the answers you will ever need in life and can be carried about in your bag with ease.

Whenever you have these weird stretches of time, whip out your book and get to reading.

Take notes on things that stick out to you, get ideas for what to take action on next.

Whatever you do… do NOT chalk these moments up

as "unsalvageable."

Quite the opposite.

Just as you can "nickel and dime" yourself to death by reckless spending, you can do the exact same with your time.

And the kicker is that you can get the money back! But the time is gone forever!

Chapter Four

—

F.A.Q.

L IKELY YOU HAVE TONS OF QUESTIONS, and that is just fine. Hopefully, you find the answer that you seek in the following questions below. All of these are questions that have been asked of me over the years and some that I threw in there just to provide a little help.

Either way, these will be a good reference for you.

Q: How do I use this book?

A: Easy! If I were to pick the best place for you to start for you to get the most practical use, it would be in chapter 3. This is where all of the tactics are listed out. If you are not super big into reading, then start here.

Pick two or three tactics that resonate with you the most and start implementing them TODAY!

—

Q: What is the best tactic to beat procrastination?

A: Well… it depends. And I know that is not the answer you are looking for, but it happens to be the best one I can give because I don't personally know you.

Here's the deal, these tactics aren't going to be for

everyone. There will be some that work wonders for you, but for John Smith next door, he thinks that they are full of crap and happens to like the one or two that you think is complete hogwash!

The best piece of advice I can give is read through them all. The one that is likely going to work best for you is probably going to have two components to it.

It sparks a "light bulb" moment for you.
It takes very little energy to get started.

Both are critical. You need to have the realization that this could work, AND you need to be able to start on it IMMEDIATELY!

Q: Is procrastination a mental disorder?

A: That is kind of difficult to answer. Since I am not a psychologist, I have to say that I cannot make any attempt to diagnose any kind of mental disorder.

Now, that being said, a preponderance of people throughout the world suffer from procrastination, but I do not believe that it is medically classified as a mental disorder.

It has been linked to other mental disorders, however.

If you do believe that you have some kind of mental disorder and you believe that procrastination is playing a large part in that, then you may consider getting professional help.

Q: Are there any positives to procrastination?

A: Yes!! Oftentimes, when we procrastinate, we are attempting to cope with something stressful. Therefore, procrastination can be a form of stress relief. And in most cases, that is exactly what it is.

—

Q: How do I know if I am a procrastinator?

A: Well… chances are, if you are reading this book, you probably already have a good idea.

I would argue that if you are reading this material, then you have recognized that you have a problem getting things accomplished, and therefore I would classify you as a procrastinator.

Q: Do you still procrastinate?

A: Of course! But because I have employed the tactics that have been listed in this book, I have yet to go a day where I do not get something done that moves the needle on the goals that I still want to accomplish.

—

Q: When I try to accomplish tasks that I have been putting off for a long time, I get really stressed. Why is that?

A: This could happen for a number of reasons. One could be that you are trying to do too much at once. But more than likely it is just a normal response to changing your habits.

For so long now, you have gotten in the routine of putting off tasks that you know need to get done, and you have not.

Once you make the shift to actually accomplishing these things, you have introduced a change into your life. A good change, for sure! But nonetheless, you will still feel the stress of change as you are forcing yourself to do something that it is not used to doing.

That being said, I still feel anxious every time I sit down to work. I chalk it up just as the price of success, which I will gladly pay to change my life and accomplish my goals.

BUT again, if you have some kind of chronic anxiety attacks or depression, I would advise you to seek professional help. No need to constantly suffer.

Q: I've tried your methods, but they don't work. What is wrong with me?

A: Probably nothing. You are human. And because you are human, you are going to have flaws. Flaws that include deviating and stopping and still procrastinating.

This is a process. My life changed radically, but I still had (and have) relapses into procrastination fits. That is just life.

The key for you is to pick a couple tactics and make a consistent and diligent effort each and every day to follow through on those tactics until they become habit. This will take time. And there will be instances where you don't want to do it. But it is in these moments when it becomes the most important for you to follow through.

I believe that the reason people find great success in their lives is really only due to a handful of things that that person does well consistently. As in, each and every day!

Q: How can I help my child to stop procrastinating on their homework?

A: This is a hard one for me. I do not have kids yet, so it is hard for me to give any kind of credible advice.

If I were to guess, I would say that you need to be the one to clean up their environment from distractions (electronics and such) since you are the adult. I can almost promise they will not do it on their own.

Just structure their surroundings as best as possible so as to facilitate them actually starting their homework.

I hear the little boogers also learn from watching their parents, so I'd say make sure you are walking the walk before you try and get them to do the same.

But again, I am speaking purely from inexperience in that department.

Q: Why is procrastination so hard to change?

A: Well, it is an emotional response to a stressful situation. Any time you deal with emotions, it will always be difficult to deal with.

And also, at a certain point, procrastination becomes habitual. And once something is a habit, it takes an act of God to change it. But that does not mean that you are forever screwed. Quite the opposite.

Remember, even though there are structural reasons in the brain for procrastination, they can be fixed. Just as habits can also be changed.

I know of many people that have broken their smoking habit and even a few that were addicted to hard drugs. They have changed. You can too.

Q: What will happen if I don't do this now?

A: Likely nothing will change for you.

Ultimately the choice is yours. And you do have a choice. I have given you the tools. Now you have to be the one to take action.

And those that take action IMMEDIATELY, as in, as soon as they finish reading this book, are typically the ones that have the best results.

So, don't stack the odds against you. Take the initiative, rip off the band-aid and just start!

If you don't change your habits and your actions, I can almost guarantee that your life will not change either.

Chapter Five

—

Conclusion

K EEP IN MIND, I am no different than you. In many respects, I am probably quite worse. I can be terribly crude at times; my manners aren't all that great (sorry mom) and I have my sinful indulgences.

However, even though I worked my way through the majority of my twenties like a leach seeking its next meal (anyone who I could bum off of), I managed to pull myself up by my bootstraps and actually make something out of my life.

Here's the thing, you are NOT doomed to a sucky, average life of sub-par achievement. You can be all that you allow yourself to be. And it starts TODAY!

Take the advice I have given you. Re-read my personal story. Understand that I SUCKED at life until I began to take the initiative to kill my procrastination demons.

And now here I stand (sit?), writing to you from the greener pastures that I have placed myself in to tell you that this can be you. This point in time, right now, can be the starting point of the rest of your life.

It can be as awesome as you choose to make it, or you can read this and not do a damn thing. And that is the cold, hard, BRUTAL truth…

Action is the determining factor. That and a little bit of the "d-word," – DISCIPLINE.

By just showing up each and every day, you give yourself a chance. And that is all you need—because a wise man once told me that life favors those in constant motion. Which explains a lot!

All these years, I have wasted watching Netflix, surfing the internet, finding company in the bottom of a beer mug and wasting all of my potential on things that, quite frankly, just do not matter one iota.

And I HATED myself for it. But I also learned a lot about myself. Maybe this will help you as well. I wasn't going to share this but, what the hell. It should help out:

These tactics work. That is the bottom line. But there is a small caveat to it. You have to WANT them to work.

I wanted them to work. But not at first. In fact, I had come to realize that I was scared. No. TERRIFIED. Terrified that if I actually did try to apply myself, that I would come to realize that I truly wasn't worth a shot of powder. I didn't want to face the possibility that I was just a lowly human being that would never amount to anything.

At least if I took that excuse, I would not have to apply myself and then I would still be able to at least believe that the possibility of me being great would still exist.

But if I truly tried. And then truly failed. I would have confirmed my greatest fear that I just wasn't good enough.

I tell you this because I found out something else… Those were all lies that kept my potential tethered like an elephant chained to a stake at a circus. Don't let this be you.

Because once you do start to succeed, once you do begin to kill the procrastination demons, you will begin to realize that this whole success thing really isn't that difficult. In fact, once you start to get a little momentum going in your favor, your self-confidence begins to skyrocket. At this point, you begin to believe you can conquer everything.

I am not the only one that realized this.

I have heard of a story of a man struggling to make it big. Like me (and probably like you, as well) he started off with plenty of challenges. Plenty of the odds stacked against him. In fact, he struggled for years to finally break the barrier of making 1 million dollars per year. Once he finally did it, the next 5 million came the following year.

But wouldn't it take 5 times as long for him to make 5 million? Shouldn't it have taken him many more years?

I thought so too. But when asked this question he smiled and responded that once he had the belief that he could be a millionaire, the rest of it was easy!

And THAT is the key. Do you believe you break through to the next level? Do you believe that you can crush your procrastination habit?

You have to.

The choice is yours. But as soon as you commit to just one or two of the tactics that I have listed above and couple that with a new belief system, your life will begin to change.

As Jim Rohn States:

"You can't alter your destination overnight, but you can change the direction of your life overnight."

Always choose to strike a new path. A path that leads to riches, relationships, and unadulterated success!

I believe in you. I know that you can do it. But all that matters is that YOU start to believe it as well.

The choice rests in your capable hands.

"You may delay, but time will not."
-Benjamin Franklin

"Only put off until tomorrow what you are willing to die having left undone."
- Pablo Picasso

"A year from now you may wish you had started today."
-Karen Lamb

"You cannot escape the responsibility of tomorrow by evading it today."
-Abraham Lincoln

"My advice is never do tomorrow what you can do today. Procrastination is the thief of time. Collar him!"
-Charles Dickens

"A day can really slip by when you're deliberately avoiding what you're supposed to do."

-Bill Watterson

"... the best possible way to prepare for tomorrow is to concentrate with all your intelligence, all your enthusiasm, on doing today's work superbly today. That is the only possible way you can prepare for the future."

-Dale Carnegie

"Someday is not a day of the week."

-Janet Dailey

16398286R00085

Printed in Great Britain
by Amazon